QUEEN LATIFAH

QUEEN LATIFAH

Sarah R. Bloom

CHELSEA HOUSE PUBLISHERS
Philadelphia

Dedication:
For my daughter Sophia—Never let anyone treat you as less than
    royalty.
For my parents—Thank you for treating me like a queen even when
    I did not act like one.

Chelsea House Publishers

Editor in Chief	Sally Cheney
Director of Production	Kim Shinners
Production Manager	Pamela Loos
Art Director	Sara Davis
Production Editor	Diann Grasse

Staff for QUEEN LATIFAH

Senior Editor	John Ziff
Associate Art Director	Takeshi Takahashi
Layout	21st Century Publishing and Communications

The Chelsea House World Wide Web address is
http://www.chelseahouse.com

3 5 7 9 8 6 4

CIP applied for ISBN 0-7910-6287-2

CONTENTS

BLACK AMERICANS OF ACHIEVEMENT

HENRY AARON
baseball great

KAREEM ABDUL-JABBAR
basketball great

MUHAMMAD ALI
heavyweight champion

RICHARD ALLEN
religious leader and social activist

MAYA ANGELOU
author

LOUIS ARMSTRONG
musician

ARTHUR ASHE
tennis great

JOSEPHINE BAKER
entertainer

TYRA BANKS
model

BENJAMIN BANNEKER
scientist and mathematician

COUNT BASIE
bandleader and composer

ANGELA BASSETT
actress

ROMARE BEARDEN
artist

HALLE BERRY
actress

MARY MCLEOD BETHUNE
educator

GEORGE WASHINGTON
CARVER
botanist

JOHNNIE COCHRAN
lawyer

BILL COSBY
entertainer

MILES DAVIS
musician

FREDERICK DOUGLASS
abolitionist editor

CHARLES DREW
physician

PAUL LAURENCE DUNBAR
poet

DUKE ELLINGTON
bandleader and composer

RALPH ELLISON
author

JULIUS ERVING
basketball great

LOUIS FARRAKHAN
political activist

ELLA FITZGERALD
singer

ARETHA FRANKLIN
entertainer

MORGAN FREEMAN
actor

MARCUS GARVEY
black nationalist leader

JOSH GIBSON
baseball great

WHOOPI GOLDBERG
entertainer

DANNY GLOVER
actor

CUBA GOODING JR.
actor

ALEX HALEY
author

PRINCE HALL
social reformer

JIMI HENDRIX
musician

MATTHEW HENSON
explorer

GREGORY HINES
performer

BILLIE HOLIDAY
singer

LENA HORNE
entertainer

WHITNEY HOUSTON
singer and actress

LANGSTON HUGHES
poet

JANET JACKSON
musician

JESSE JACKSON
civil-rights leader and politician

MICHAEL JACKSON
entertainer

SAMUEL L. JACKSON
actor

T. D. JAKES
religious leader

JACK JOHNSON
heavyweight champion

MAE JEMISON
astronaut

MAGIC JOHNSON
basketball great

SCOTT JOPLIN
composer

BARBARA JORDAN
politician

MICHAEL JORDAN
basketball great

CORETTA SCOTT KING
civil-rights leader

MARTIN LUTHER KING, JR.
civil-rights leader

LEWIS LATIMER
scientist

SPIKE LEE
filmmaker

CARL LEWIS
champion athlete

RONALD MCNAIR
astronaut

MALCOLM X
militant black leader

BOB MARLEY
musician

THURGOOD MARSHALL
Supreme Court justice

TERRY MCMILLAN
author

TONI MORRISON
author

ELIJAH MUHAMMAD
religious leader

EDDIE MURPHY
entertainer

JESSE OWENS
champion athlete

SATCHEL PAIGE
baseball great

CHARLIE PARKER
musician

ROSA PARKS
civil-rights leader

COLIN POWELL
military leader

QUEEN LATIFAH
entertainer

DELLA REESE
entertainer

PAUL ROBESON
singer and actor

JACKIE ROBINSON
baseball great

CHRIS ROCK
comedian and actor

DIANA ROSS
entertainer

AL SHARPTON
minister and activist

WILL SMITH
actor

WESLEY SNIPES
actor

CLARENCE THOMAS
Supreme Court justice

SOJOURNER TRUTH
antislavery activist

HARRIET TUBMAN
antislavery activist

NAT TURNER
slave revolt leader

TINA TURNER
entertainer

ALICE WALKER
author

MADAM C. J. WALKER
entrepreneur

BOOKER T. WASHINGTON
educator

DENZEL WASHINGTON
actor

J. C. WATTS
politician

VANESSA WILLIAMS
singer and actress

VENUS WILLIAMS
tennis star

OPRAH WINFREY
entertainer

TIGER WOODS
golf star

ON ACHIEVEMENT

————— ❧ —————

Coretta Scott King

Before you begin this book, I hope you will ask yourself what the word *excellence* means to you. I think it's a question we should all ask, and keep asking as we grow older and change. Because the truest answer to it should never change. When you think of excellence, perhaps you think of success at work; or of becoming wealthy; or meeting the right person, getting married, and having a good family life.

Those goals are worth striving for, but there is a better way to look at excellence. As Martin Luther King Jr. said in one of his last sermons, "I want you to be first in love. I want you to be first in moral excellence. I want you to be first in generosity. If you want to be important, wonderful. If you want to be great, wonderful. But recognize that he who is greatest among you shall be your servant."

My husband knew that the true meaning of achievement is service. When I met him, in 1952, he was already ordained as a Baptist minister and was working toward a doctoral degree at Boston University. I was studying at the New England Conservatory and dreamed of accomplishments in music. We married a year later, and after I graduated the following year we moved to Montgomery, Alabama. We didn't know it then, but our notions of achievement were about to undergo a dramatic change.

You may have read or heard about what happened next. What began with the boycott of a local bus line grew into a national crusade, and by the time he was assassinated in 1968 my husband had fashioned a black movement powerful enough to shatter forever the practice of racial segregation. What you may not have read about is where he learned to resist injustice without compromising his religious beliefs.

He adopted a strategy of nonviolence from a man of a different race, who lived in a different country and even practiced a different religion. The man was Mahatma Gandhi, the great leader of India, who devoted his life to serving humanity in the spirit of love and nonviolence. It was in these principles that Martin discovered his method for social reform. More than anything else, those two principles were the key to his achievements.

These books are about African Americans who served society through the excellence of their achievements. They form part of the rich history of black men and women in America—a history of stunning accomplishments in every field of human endeavor, from literature and art to science, industry, education, diplomacy, athletics, jurisprudence, even polar exploration.

Not all of the people in this history had the same ideals, but I think you will find that all of them had something in common. Like Martin Luther King Jr., they all decided to become "drum majors" and serve humanity. In that principle—whether it was expressed in books, inventions, or song—they found a goal and a guide outside themselves that showed them a way to serve others instead of living only for themselves.

Reading the stories of these courageous men and women not only helps us discover the principles that we will use to guide our own lives; it also teaches us about our black heritage and about America itself. It is crucial for us to know the heroes and heroines of our history and to realize that the price we paid in our struggle for equality in America was dear. But we must also understand that we have gotten as far as we have partly because America's democratic system and ideals made it possible.

We are still struggling with racism and prejudice. But the great men and women in this series are a tribute to the spirit of the country in which they have flourished. And that makes their stories special and worth knowing.

1

LETTING GO

❦

THE SPRING OF 1992 marked the 22nd birthday of Dana Owens, to be better known some time later as Queen Latifah. She had recently released her second album, *Nature of a Sista'*, had been nominated for a Grammy for previous work, and had just appeared in Spike Lee's *Jungle Fever*. Fame was coming quickly to the young rapper, and her family and friends were there to cheer her on. She had just bought a home in New Jersey with the dream of having her mother Rita and her brother Lance, known as "Winki," live with her. Traveling for concerts and the responsibilities of stardom took their toll on her energy; Latifah did not want to waste her precious time at home traveling to visit her mother in one place and her brother in another.

Tragically, that dream of having her family together in one house again would not come true. Shortly after her birthday, Queen Latifah was helping her good friend Latee maneuver a couch up to his second-floor apartment. The move took a lot of effort and several hours. Finally they were finished; she, Latee, and their friends who had helped could relax. Then the call came, a 911 page from her friend Ramsey.

There are moments in a person's life that, in hindsight, are seen as turning points. They are often

At 22, everything seemed to be going great for Queen Latifah. She had received a Grammy nomination and had appeared in Spike Lee's film Jungle Fever. *But the sudden and tragic death of her brother "Winki" in a motorcycle accident tore her apart with grief.*

marked by an emotional extreme, joy or sorrow, which plants the seed for growth. How one deals with that experience can determine the path one's life may take, as well as one's character. In that spring of 1992, the words that came over the telephone marked perhaps the greatest turning point in the life of Queen Latifah. "Your brother had an accident on his motorcycle," she heard, and the fork in the road appeared just over the horizon.

Her friend Shakim rushed her to the hospital; Latifah knew that she was too upset even to find the hospital. As they maneuvered through the traffic, a storm thundered and poured rain down on them as if to signal the long sadness that was soon to surround her. The rain was slowing them down even more—all she could do was to pray that he would be okay—and remind herself to breathe. Then she saw it—the twisted motorcycle lying on a tow truck bed. It had been her gift to her brother on his birthday just a few months before. Even as her heart sank, her mind reached out to the hope that he might have jumped off before the crash.

The doctors worked on him for countless hours, it seemed. They manually massaged his heart and gave him pint after pint of blood. Latifah, her mother, and friends waited in a silence broken only by the soft sound of crying and praying. Eventually, however, the devastating news came, "I'm sorry, but we lost him," and the family had to accept that 24-year-old Winki was gone.

In her 1999 autobiography, *Ladies First,* Queen Latifah describes the intense pain she felt upon losing her brother, "It would be months before I would finally accept Winki's death. Every morning and every evening, my grief pounded at my skull, tearing through my heart. Losing Winki was like losing half of myself. I was numb and empty."

She had bought the motorcycle—a Kawasaki Ninja ZX7—for her brother on his 24th birthday, but it was he who had sparked her interest in bikes in the first place. It had become their thing together; other good friends in her "posse" would acquire motorcycles and soon they were all riding together, thriving on the freedom they felt. It was a long while before Latifah was able to get back on her bike after Winki's death. In time, she would put the key to her brother's bike on a gold chain to wear forever. Once, after having moved to Los Angeles for her TV series, she set out for the road in the middle of the night and had her ride, feeling Winki's presence that she longed for so desperately.

Dana Owens grew up with Winki always near; all the bonds in her immediate family were strong, but the tie between her and Winki was especially strong. Her mother continuously gave her encouragement to be herself and her father never let her feel that she could not do something because she was a girl. Still it remained her brother from whom her greatest strengths arose and this continues, unbroken even by his death. He watches over her still—her guardian angel.

Born Lancelot Owens Jr., Latifah's brother soon became Winki. Their mother Rita said th~ when he woke from napping, he often had c· stuck closed. She would ask if he were · her, calling him her "little Winki," an stayed with him into adulthood—even became a police officer. Rita and the separated in 1978, leaving Winki to be the their house wherever they would live.

As Latifah struggled with the death of her brother, she continued to work on her successful TV show, Living Single. Here—with costars Erika Alexander, Kim Fields, and Kim Coles—Latifah wears the key to her brother's motorcycle on a chain around her neck.

While their mother never said anything negative about her husband Lance, the children knew he was cheating on her and was involved with drugs. Latifah's brother became the example of the good man in her life. In her autobiography, she describes the relationship:

Winki was one of my best friends, but not because he was my brother. . . . He always pushed me to be and do my best. He was the only man in my life who was there for me one hundred percent, who loved me unconditionally—no strings, no expectations, just straight-up love. . . . Winki was the one constant friend in my life. Not only was he the man of the house after my parents split up, but he was also my protector and my soul mate.

In the months that followed Winki's death, Queen Latifah was wracked by guilt and grief. Her instincts were to blame God; her impulse was to join Winki in death. But her best friend Tammy refused to let her blame God. Tammy herself had known grief; only three years earlier, she had lost her mother to cancer. Thus, she was able to share Latifah's grief. Though the numbness stayed with Latifah, gradually with Tammy's support and her own deep faith in God, she found the strength to emerge from her downward spiral of despair.

Shortly before the accident that took her brother's life, Queen Latifah's contract negotiations with Tommy Boy records had fallen apart, and she had agreed to record her third album, *Black Reign,* with Motown. With her recovery beginning, she remembered her obligations to her work. When she felt she could not manage, she turned to Winki:

> So I talked with Winki. And then I found that being around music and listening to the songs that Winki and I shared was therapeutic. Suddenly, my focus shifted. I poured myself into my music. I lived in the studio. Winki helped me write *Black Reign*. I became obsessed with finishing the album. It had become about survival.

Latifah's brother Winki kept her head above water innumerable times. She had begun to lean on marijuana and was having difficulty emerging from her zombie-like state. In *Black Reign* (1993), she found a way to express the deepest parts of her soul and to experience release from pain for a little while:

> I could choose to wallow in my pain and grief, or I could choose to get up and get through it. The choice was mine. I couldn't blame anybody or expect anyone to pick myself up for me. Things happen. But what are you going to do when they happen to you?

For Latifah, the album is the most personal of her albums for obvious reasons. She has found that audiences often cry with her when she performs the song "Winki's Theme." In it, she found a way to express the deepest parts of her soul, and to experience release from pain for a little while.

The album has also been her biggest success to date, with the single "U.N.I.T.Y." going on to win a Grammy Award. Her exposure broadened and the critics loved her. In 1994 *The Source* wrote, "out of the sea of bland and repetitive rap albums currently nailing the coffin shut on the legacy of funk comes a welcome life raft of sanity." Latifah's strength of character was also reemerging in 1994, and her heart and soul began to shine through. More struggles would follow, however, before she could recognize the long-term effects that her brother's death would have on her, her music, and her beliefs.

After the release of *Black Reign*, Queen Latifah was offered the role of Khadijah in *Living Single*; her acceptance meant, however, that she had to move to Los Angeles. Working on the TV series helped her get through each day, but she would continue to struggle for years before she felt able to release her grief and think of Winki without sinking into depression and guilt.

Her music and her belief in God would sustain her and eventually teach her to be free of the burden she carried and to recognize the inner strength that began in those first days following Winki's death. Getting through to a place of letting go is how Latifah began to deal with obstacles in life. She writes in her autobiography that faith in God is the beginning:

At the 1995 Soul Train Music Awards, Latifah was honored with the Sammy Davis Jr. Award for Entertainer of the Year.

In her rise to fame, Latifah has overcome many obstacles and experienced many joys. Here she joins fellow rapper Eve on stage to celebrate the opening of Black Entertainment Television's new Harlem-based studios.

Being spiritual isn't about being perfect. The Lord knows I'm not perfect. To me, being spiritual is recognizing that we aren't necessarily operating on our own steam. And that ultimately, not everything in this life is under our control.

We have to let go and let God do His job. But first, we have to have faith.

Queen Latifah would increasingly wear the title of royalty ever more proudly and with greater purpose—her vision clearer, her beauty more vibrant, and her humanity brighter than ever.

2

BORN A QUEEN

❧

D ANA ELAINE OWENS seemed to want a grand entrance even for her birth. After 10 long months for her mother Rita, she finally came out on March 18, 1970, weighing in at 8 pounds, 3 ounces. From the beginning, her mother noticed how much energy her new baby had, and as Dana grew older, her mother saw that her daughter was not a personality to be stopped. She always wanted to get involved in everything, including things that her mother did not recognize as of interest to girls. Yet Rita never made her feel as if her interests were strange or wrong in any way.

At three years old she took karate lessons because her brother was learning, and her father encouraged her to be just as good. A little older and she wanted ballet and guitar lessons. Her mother, not wanting to have her daughter hear the word "no" because of money problems, did some research and found a community center at which Dana could have inexpensive lessons. The center charge was set according to a family's income.

No matter what difficulties she had financially or personally, she always thought of Dana and Winki first, making sure their opportunities were equal to those of other kids. From the experience of her own struggles, Rita Bray Owens knew that those opportunities would help to support the kind of inner

Born Dana Owens, Queen Latifah has always had a close relationship with her mother, Rita Owens. Rita continually encouraged her daughter to believe in herself, a fact Latifah credits for her self-confidence today.

strength she wanted her children to have. She made it a point to recognize their personalities and then set out to nurture those qualities and encourage them to be true to their own talents and ideals. Looking back in her autobiography, Latifah writes:

> She laid the foundation for me to become a self-proclaimed queen. She made the ground fertile for me to persevere, no matter what the obstacles, and to keep my head up. My mother always told me how smart, beautiful, and talented I was. In her mind, there was nothing I couldn't do. . . . She never limited me. My mother believed in me before I even believed in myself. And because of that, no one can shake my confidence now.

The things Rita did to guide her children took effect very early, as an incident when Dana was only five years old illustrates. One day in kindergarten, she was accidentally locked out of the school after recess. Realizing that she could not get in, she began walking to the place she knew was closest and most safe—her grandmother's house. This was, however, a mile and a half walk through busy intersections; yet somehow this tough five-year-old girl made it there, though she gave her family quite a scare. Her mother, relieved that her baby was okay, recognized something in Dana that has blossomed in her adulthood—that she was resourceful and not afraid to face any situation that came her way.

Another way in which Rita helped Dana develop into the remarkable woman known as Queen Latifah was to be open to dialogue, communication that Rita had lacked with her own parents. By not judging and by taking the time to listen to what her children had to say, she gained their trust even more than simply as a mother, and they were more likely to go to her not just with problems, but also the everyday details that a mother might not normally get to hear. In the foreword to Latifah's autobiography, Rita wrote, "The best way I could protect her was by showing her how to stick up for herself. I knew that she was going to run into a lot of battles in her years—because that's life—and I wanted her to see right from the start that she could take them on."

Dana's father, Lancelot Owens, was also a strong source of support. He never made Dana feel different or less than her brother because she was a girl. A Viet Nam veteran and a police officer for the city of Newark, he tried to be a protector as well as a companion to his children.

The first time he took them camping, Dana was six years old and Winki was eight. Rain poured throughout the entire weekend. Rather than herding them back home, their father decreed they would stay since there was still plenty to do despite the rain. He got them up early to see an almost invisible sun rising in the east, they made campfires with the driest wood they could find and watched their dad cooking, and they traipsed through the woods looking for nature's signals, such as the north identifiable by where moss was growing on a tree. Latifah's father taught her that even when life is not the way you want it, you can go on living and finding enjoyment. What looked like a ruined weekend at the beginning, the rain coming down without a halt, their father turned into opportunity. "Hey," he told his children, "life's not always going to be sunshine every day. What are you gonna do when there are a few clouds? You have to keep going." She has carried this lesson with her.

As her father, Lance also gave Latifah a sense of royalty through the love and affection he showered on her. He made her feel strong and proud to be who she was and to believe she could tackle anything that came her way. He encouraged Dana to be an equal to her brother, never separating their activities, and this support helped bolster her self-confidence tremendously. Even while going through his own difficulties, he never let his daughter or son feel that he was not available; he took them out for dinner, continued to

Although her parents split up when Latifah was a child, both are enthusiastic supporters of her achievements today. Latifah's father (center) is a Viet Nam vet and a former Newark, New Jersey, police officer.

give them karate lessons, and whenever they called, he was always ready to talk on the phone with them.

One example of how Latifah saw her father occurred when she was seven years old. Her parents took the two children shopping in the city; on the way back, they passed a man screaming at a woman whom he was slapping again and again across the face. The horrified Latifah and Winki begged their father to do something. But they didn't have to ask. Even though he was off duty, Owens jumped from the car and drew his police gun on the man so that the woman could get away. While he held the man, he told him in strong terms that real men do not manhandle a woman. Then he let the man go. In her father Latifah found a protecting yet loving force that complemented her mother's nurturing side.

But her father's behavior with drugs, alcohol, and women shook her and her brother's confidence and hurt them; as children they preferred to focus on daddy-as-superhero. As an adult, however, Latifah learned to recognize that her father had problems that were to some degree responsible for what she and Winki did not love in him, pain arising from what he had seen and done in Viet Nam and as a police officer. Although his duty required killings, still they were a heavy burden to carry. During that time, however, even after he began to be consistently involved with the drugs and affairs and Rita took the kids and left him, neither he nor Rita ever spoke disparagingly of each other in front of the children. Both parents made every effort to be certain that Winki and Latifah always felt safe and loved. This is a gift Dana recognizes today as unique.

Only much later did Queen Latifah and her brother find out about their father's infidelities, including the children he had fathered with other women. The damage to the esteem that she once held for her father was the most difficult to overcome. The loss of respect and the impact the knowledge had on her feelings about men in general were worse for her than learning that she had a half sister only two years younger whom she had never seen. Latifah, however, made the choice to work on that relationship rather than turn her back on her father:

> I . . . decided that I do still need my father in my life. I looked at what I *could* control. I wanted to make a choice to have him in my life. I could decide to forgive him and to forge the bond that we hadn't had since those days when he and Winki and I went camping.
>
> More than anything, I wanted to stop living in the past, because I could not change it.

After Winki's death, Lance Sr. would seek help for his drug and alcohol problems, as well as his grief, and their relationship has strengthened. Latifah has also developed close relationships with her half brother and sisters, Angelo, Michelle, and Kelly. Michelle, two years younger than Latifah, did not meet their father until she was 17 years old. From her aunt and her good friend Monifa, one of whom had her husband leave and the other her father die when she was nine, Latifah came to understand that she was lucky still to have a father with whom she could be angry.

If her father's weakness seems to have encouraged her impulse to be strong, she also had the desire to reveal the softer part of her nature. In 1978, when she was eight years old, she changed her name to Latifah. She and her cousin Sharonda were looking through a book of Muslim names. At the time, it was becoming very popular for African Americans to give them-selves a Muslim name in the tradition of Malcolm X and the Nation of Islam. The Civil Rights movement spawned the desire by blacks in this country to reclaim the culture that slavery had stripped away. The Muslim names were meant to show pride in their heritage and to reject the European names that were considered slave names.

Sharonda had already chosen, calling herself Salima Wadiah, which means "safe and healthy," and then it was Dana's turn. Her brother Winki had also taken a Muslim name, Jameel, which means "beautiful." Seeing the name "Latifah," she knew it would be her name. It sounded right, and when she read the meaning next to the name in the book, she knew it described her deepest nature: "delicate, sensitive, kind." That was the person Dana was, and Latifah was born.

Even though other kids had teased her for being a tomboy throughout her childhood, and even though she shunned fancy bows, ribbons, and dresses when she played in the mud and on the basketball courts, Latifah was a very sensitive soul inside. She

often cried to her mother about the taunting and she felt slights deeply. It was partly the desire to show the outside world a little more of her inner self that led her to choose her name.

When she conferred her "Queen" title 10 years later, it was somewhat redundant. Her attitude of self-confidence and her radiant beauty made her seem like a queen long before she adopted the name itself.

Her mother was the greatest influence in fostering the royalty in her. When her parents split up, her mother had no choice except to move Latifah and Winki into the Hyatt Court housing project because

When she was eight years old, Dana chose the name Latifah from a book of Muslim names. At the time, the tradition of Malcolm X (seen speaking at a rally in New York in the 1960s) and the Nation of Islam movement inspired many African Americans to take Muslim names as a way to reclaim a sense of identity.

of her low income. Rather than rage at the misfortune and at the surroundings, Rita did not waste emotion on anger or self-pity, nor let her children indulge in these attitudes. She took on a third job so that there would be no deprivation for her children and especially not for Latifah. Rita had discovered that Dana's scores on national tests placed her among the intellectually gifted, so gifted that she was able to skip a grade.

Rita spent much of her energies on teaching her children to recognize what happens to people who become negative, who wallow in self-pity and have no intention of moving up and out of the projects. She wanted to make sure Latifah and Winki evaded that trap, that they knew the low-income housing was a stepping-stone, and a positive one at that.

Surrounded by poverty, Rita transformed their apartment into a home. She decorated with bright fabrics and beautiful smells, potpourri by the front door so that her children came home to wonderful scents and colorful fabrics that lifted their spirits the moment they saw them. Their home did not look like the project. She knew that nurturing pride in one's space is a springboard that encourages pride in oneself, and Rita gave this to her children. Winki and Dana were encouraged to decorate their own rooms in whatever manner they chose, giving them the confidence to express their personalities and the freedom to do so. Dana centered her room around music even at age eight, making sure there was a big open space for dancing. She knew what she liked and stayed true to that.

Rita made sure her children saw her as her own person, too, after her struggles to discover herself. Growing up as the middle daughter of seven children, Rita always felt defined by her relationships to others. It was not until she was a grown woman that she was able to take her love of art and make something of it. Because of her own experiences, she always took time out to express her own needs and explain them.

Respect needs to be earned, and their mother earned it repeatedly.

Their time in the projects is not a time of bad memories for Queen Latifah. Rita had made it very clear that it was merely a stopover. "Look," she told them, "you're black; you're already at a disadvantage. . . . You have to work twice as hard to make it. So don't get comfortable here." She was determined they should not accept Hyatt Court as their world, no matter how attractive she had made it. So that they could experience the better world that she intended they keep their eyes on, she sent them to

After Latifah's parents split up, she moved with her mother and brother to a housing project in Newark. Although money was tight, Latifah's mother Rita made a loving home for her children in the project.

her mother's family in Virginia or Maryland for parts of the summers so that they could remember there was more than the courtyard of their building. Down south they stayed in a house surrounded by land—lots of it—and they swam in clean pools and they ate huge meals every night.

To Latifah, a great part of the happiness she experienced there came from her wonderful family. At her Grandma Bray's house, filled with aunts and uncles and cousins, Latifah found a very receptive audience before whom to practice her performing. She entertained them by imitating different accents—Jamaican and Spanish—and she mimicked acts she saw on television and songs she heard on the radio.

Returning to Hyatt Court, she and her brother were very aware of the differences between them and the other children who had to stay in the projects all summer. Latifah and Winki had no interest in hanging out in the courtyard doing nothing; rather, they were always searching for fun. That search took them to the recreation center where they could play Ping-Pong and cards and other games. The courtyard, while always buzzing with a lot of people, was boring to them.

Their mother also organized field trips for their building, trying to show the children the world outside their cement building. They took buses to the Bronx Zoo or the Jersey shore, and she encouraged them to look at the world through windows other than Hyatt Court. When Rita began taking classes at Kean College to become an art teacher, she took the children along, exposing them to yet another new experience. Seeing her mother go back to school, after having given up that dream to have a family with her husband, also inspired Dana. Her mother consistently did whatever was necessary to improve her conditions, without complaining and without sacrificing her children's welfare.

Her two years of working three jobs would

finally provide enough money for a down payment on a small house in Newark, but she needed a $40,000 mortgage from the bank in order to buy it. She was rejected because she had no credit history. She had never bought anything on credit. Rather than considering how much she had saved in that short time or that she had managed her money so well that she had not had to borrow, banks considered only that she was divorced, black, and a woman. Refusing to succumb to discouragement,

Always eager to share the gifts of her experience and prosperity, Latifah (joined here by her mother) frequently appears at special events, like this one for local high school students at the New Jersey Performing Arts Center in Newark.

Rita kept her promise and found an apartment in a residential area of Newark. They moved into a three-family house; the entire second floor was theirs—and it was massive in the eyes of Latifah and Winki! Not only that, they had a large back-yard as a bonus.

As Latifah grew up, her mother and brother were the biggest influences in her life. Her mother gave her the freedom always to speak the truth. Thus, the lines of communication were always open between them. When Latifah received her first kiss at 11, she told her mother about it, and it was her mother's ability to listen that allowed Latifah to tell her details. Rita hid her relief when Latifah described the soft, single kiss on the cheek.

Her brother always pushed her to do more, to be better and smarter than she already was. Constantly egging her on, he urged her to try new things, some-times getting her into trouble, but teaching her to push her way through any fears. When he was older, he took very seriously the responsibilities of being "man of the house." He found an after-school job so that he could contribute to household expenses, and even gave allowance money to Latifah. She marveled at her big brother's willingness to help out and give her money when he did not have to.

In 1984, now a sophomore, Latifah transferred to Irvington High School, where her mother had taught art classes since 1981. At her previous school, St. Anne's, she had performed in a produc-tion of *The Wiz* when she was in the 7th grade. Her singing in the role of Dorothy brought a standing ovation from an audience with tears in their eyes at the beauty of her voice.

At Irvington she entered a talent competition. She was fearful about performing on stage and somewhat nervous at the new school, but she had been given such strength and confidence from her family and from that first experience that she knew she could walk out there anyway, regardless of the fear. She sang a song by Luther Vandross and once more an audience rose for a standing ovation when she was done. Her self-assurance was raised another level. She now describes dealing with fear in this way:

> There's nothing wrong with being afraid. There *is* something wrong—definitely wrong—with being so afraid that you don't even try. I've always been more afraid of *not* trying something. If you try and fail, at least you know what you can't do, and it leaves you room to attempt something else and keep going for it until you find your niche. But, if you never try, that's the biggest failure.

Having the confidence to overcome one's fears has been one of Queen Latifah's biggest assets. It has helped her get past difficulties that would have trapped many others. When she was just 15 years old, playing basketball as the star forward for Irvington High, she became involved in a sexual relationship with Raheem, a 24-year-old man who helped coach the team. Latifah quickly recognized that he was taking advantage of her youth, telling her she was beautiful and everything else she wanted to hear. She also realized that she had been using him, thinking that being with a man would make her a woman. She broke it off, having learned that few ever become a woman that way.

Unfortunately, it took more convincing to have faith in her own thinking when no one else seemed to know what she had discovered for herself. In the lure of being wanted, flattered by men, she would sometimes find it difficult to acknowledge to herself that she was again being exploited. Finally, a degrading episode with a 40-year-old man, whom she did not even like, reminded her of the lesson she had first learned with Raheem. Her sense of her value determined her choice—she would take care of

On the set of Living Single, *Latifah gets a chance to revisit her high school years, and have some fun, with the help of former Olympian and women's basketball star Cheryl Miller.*

her body and love it, and she did not need sex in order to feel good about herself. She only needed to look inside herself:

> I'd rather be broke than destroy my heart, than face the bottomless pit I did that night. . . . Every time you sleep with somebody, it's like you give that person a piece of your soul. Did I want this guy to have a piece of me? No. Plain and simple. But it was a long road getting there.

Experience with drugs was similar, yet briefer. She feels fortunate today that her one attempt at cocaine use led her to a terrifying vision of what her life could become, and she chose never to touch it again. She saw what drug addiction did to her father. She has a cousin who is hooked on heroin, and she has seen many others unable to break the chains of addiction, including a girl who had quit the basketball team. Latifah's intense curiosity even led her to sell drugs for one day, but the shame won out. Being able to see herself through the eyes of God and her mother helped her have the strength to be true to who she was, and that was not a drug dealer, a drug user, or a sex addict.

All these events added to her sense of self and helped her to try things she felt her soul drawn to— the world of rap and hip-hop. The Latin Quarter, a club in New York City, was booming with the sound in the mid-1980s, and Latifah wanted to be there. Rap had exploded into the world of music a few years earlier and now was already moving into a new phase with the Beastie Boys, Salt-N-Pepa, Run-D.M.C., and Grandmaster Flash.

The lure was large, the music was bumping, and Latifah's curiosity and spirited independence were too strong for anyone to be able to keep her away.

3

PRINCESS OF
THE POSSE

T HE SCENE IS New York City. The time is the
early 1980s and rap music is becoming increasingly popular. KRS-One and Public Enemy are taking rhyming to
a new level, a level in which the words mean something
powerful. This was to have a strong influence on Latifah
and her lyrics. The place to be seen is the Latin Quarter,
a club no longer in existence, located at the corner of
Forty-eighth Street and Broadway on Times Square.
Latifah is in her early teens, making trips to the Big
Apple every chance she gets—she just cannot stay away.

After long lines and getting frisked by security
before paying a $10 cover, one entered the mecca for
rap music, with rappers such as Run-D.M.C., Rakim,
and Salt-N-Pepa taking the stage and rubbing elbows
with the packed house. Latifah was in her element,
feeding off the energy and excitement and running
back to New Jersey and her friends at Irvington High
School to report all she saw and heard.

In the mid-1980s, New York City became a center for the growing world of rap and hip-hop music. The lure of the club scene continually drew Latifah into the city, where she watched and learned as up-and-coming rappers showed their skills.

Back then, nobody really left Jersey that much. But I
couldn't be kept away from New York. After my first
night in Times Square, the pulse kept pulling me back
like a magnetic force. I couldn't not be there. I was feeling
the music, the dance, the language pulsating in me. My
posse started to depend on me to bring them some New
York flavor every week, and I loved going back to them,
sharing what I had just seen. I was spreading the culture.

In 1979 The Sugar Hill Gang released a single called "Rapper's Delight" that changed the face of music, bringing rap into the commercial spotlight. The single sold millions of copies and reached the top of the pop charts. Other groups quickly began releasing singles on small record labels devoted to rap music. Rappers such as Kurtis Blow and Grandmaster Flash launched equally successful singles on the market, and the culture began to expand within the major cities.

The culture of rap involved particular clothing styles, its own dialect, and the street dancing that became known as break dancing. Rapping on the street corner and spreading graffiti "tags" (graphic depictions representing the individual or neighborhood) had begun to explode throughout urban areas, forging a bond between the African-American and Latino inner-city kids. In part, the cohesion grew out of their anger and frustration at the ongoing loss of community caused by city planning commissions that arbitrarily relocated poor families with little regard for the neighborhoods they were disrupting.

Rap music—in the parks, in the clubs, and on the streets—became a way in which the young of the inner city could communicate with one another about their shared experiences, in essentially their own language. The clothes, the style, and the method of dancing further bonded this group together. After the release of "Rapper's Delight" and its monumental success, the culture began to exceed its environs and make its way into the mainstream, slowly at first, and then like a tidal wave.

In 1985, the 15-year-old Latifah was riding the crest of that wave in New York City. In an interview with *Essence* magazine in 1999, she describes herself at that age: "I think I was born independent. My brother kind of stayed home, but I would wander out. I had a compulsive need to find out new things."

She started an all-female rap group called Ladies

In rap's early days, artists like Grandmaster Flash (left), Sugarhill Gang, and Kurtis Blow were forging a new musical style that would influence Latifah's future work.

Fresh, and they performed before the basketball games at Irvington High School and at pep rallies. Latifah wrote all her own lyrics, focusing on Afrocentric themes and experiences from childhood. Her pride in her heritage is echoed throughout her work, and it became a theme that many other rap groups adopted because of her success with it.

Latifah worked at a local Burger King to support her cultural education. Changing out of her uniform into her rapper gear from her backpack, she became herself in a sweat suit and a Benetton fishing hat. She traveled back and forth to New York and the clubs there, observing the atmosphere and absorbing the culture.

Not long after transferring to Irvington High School, she met Ramsey Gdelawoe. Her friends had told her that Ramsey was the very coolest, so she was curious to meet him. Immediately friends, she found him even more excited about the music in New York than she was. Ramsey taught Latifah all he knew about the world of rap music and introduced her to others whose love for rap matched theirs. He had been going to the hippest spots in New York and setting clothing trends at Irvington High for some time already. The Lincoln Tunnel became their avenue to the magic of the music that would not leave their souls.

As hip as Ramsey was back then, and as many dee-jays as he knew, it was Latifah's mother who introduced her to "the one deejay who would change my life" as she puts it in her book *Ladies First*. Her mother met him because she was in charge of finding deejays for the class activities, and Latifah and Mark the 45 King hit it off right away. His basement became a cauldron brewing with young rappers, eager to lay down a groove over Mark's tracks. Dana began shyly, just wanting to be a part of the scene, but her friend Ramsey pushed her to grab the mike. She started out poorly, but ever-determined, she kept trying until the sound she knew was within her came out. Mark's basement became the place to be, as Latifah describes:

> Mark's basement was always buzzing with people from the neighborhood—and eventually we became a posse. I was the only female MC in the group and the youngest, so I called myself Princess of the Posse. Down there, in the small space among Mark's equipment, the world was far away and time ceased to exist. We were about the music. . . . We wanted to know everything we could about the artists, the music, the clothes. We studied rap inside and out. Many of us eventually scored record deals simply because we were so prepared; we knew what we were getting ourselves into. It was like the training before the job.

Ramsey did not rap, but had become the surrogate big brother of the group, urging them on and dreaming big. Latifah herself did not even think of becoming a rapper. She thought of it as a hobby, and enrolled in the Borough of Manhattan Community College soon after to study broadcast journalism. Her dreams at this point were to become a lawyer or a newscaster. Rap did not seem like a viable dream—yet. Singing in the all-female rap group Ladies Fresh in high school was one thing. Being a famous rapper was quite another. It did not take long, however, for the dream to take hold.

The group Salt-N-Pepa is often credited with being the first female rap group, but in fact there were several other all-female groups and female rappers playing the clubs during this time, though all were not as noticeable. Latifah saw Salt-N-Pepa perform at the Latin Quarter for their first time and while she was excited to see women up there, she felt unable to relate to the spandex and boots the women used to show off their bodies. Standing there in her sweat suit and sneakers, she could not identify. And then she saw Sweet T and Jazzy Joyce perform—women who dressed in casual clothes and wore their hair in ponytails—and Latifah suddenly knew that she too could do it:

> I saw someone who looked like me doing something I'd only imagined doing in my sweetest, most distant dreams. Before Jazzy Joyce and Sweet T, it had never really occurred to me that *I* could be up there, rocking the house. What I needed was a role model, and watching their success grow right before my very eyes put ideas in my head. My dreams were morphing into reality up there. I started thinking, "Maybe I can do it too." Yeah. I could hear them: "Go, La-ti-fah, Go, La, Go! Give it to 'em La!"
>
> I could see it.

Latifah expanded her rap education to other clubs and venues and all-night parties in Brooklyn, much to

In New York, Latifah saw women taking center stage at clubs like the Latin Quarter. The now-famous group Salt-N-Pepa (seen here at the Grammy Awards) impressed Latifah, but she found herself looking for a more casual style.

her mother's distress. After one such night out without calling home, Latifah received a remarkable gift from the woman who had raised her. Fearful of the anger that she expected, she walked into her mother's room to take what she felt she deserved for being out all night and half the next day. To her surprise, however, her mother cried and explained that while she was unhappy that her daughter was out all night, still she was not fearful. She knew God would care for Latifah. She made it clear that God was also watching whatever her daughter was doing out there and Latifah would have to "answer to Him." For Latifah, her mother's words were the purest expression of love and faith and a lesson she carries still in her life. Her mother never had to wonder where she was after that.

Her mother—the original Queen, as Latifah calls her—has been a role model throughout the rapper's life. At Irvington High School, Rita founded the Urban Youth Coalition in 1986 in order to teach students about leadership skills and conflict resolution, as well as the importance of self-esteem and cultural diversity. She later won the Excellence in Teaching Award from New Jersey governor Christine Todd Whitman for her efforts, as well as the Role Model of the Year Award from Lincoln University.

So when Latifah came to her mother after a semester at Borough of Manhattan Community College and said she had decided to try to make it as a rapper, her mother told her to "go for it." And with the support of her family and friends, she did. She practiced in Mark's basement and formed a tight group of fellow rappers who urged one another on and gave each other strength. Ramsey was the cheerleader, dreaming bigger than any of them and assuring them that fame would be theirs.

In the summer of 1987, 17-year-old Latifah had her first song played on the radio. The words "Baseline affect me/My rhymes direct me/Forgive the crowds, oh Lord/They know not why/They sweat me" came blaring into her kitchen from her demo "Princess of the Posse," and Latifah ran back and forth from window to window in her apartment screaming to anyone who would listen that she was on the radio.

She and her friends, now calling themselves "The Flavor Unit," were on the rise and putting New Jersey on the map for the crowd at the Latin Quarter. Her friend Latee was the first of the group to be signed, and when he hit the stage, it was a monumental occurrence for the friends because it was the first tangible evidence that they could really succeed in music. Soon after Latee, two more Flavor Unit members were signed with Wild Pitch, an independent label that had recently emerged.

Then came the Queen. Ramsey gave up his rent money in order to get Latifah and D.J. Mark into a recording studio in Orange, New Jersey. After practicing in Mark's basement for so long, the recording went quickly. Latifah started it off, rapping in a Jamaican dialect—a totally unique addition at the time—and in two hours she had her first demo. "Wrath of My Madness" was on the A-side and "Princess of the Posse" was on the B-side, and they all knew it was good:

> My mellow Latee was kicking flavor
> The R.E. posse said "Yo Latifah we can do this"
> So I paused in the thought and in my brilliance
>   I caught
> And I agreed because I already knew this
> Now you should want to flex, cause I'm in full effect
> Queen Latifah is five-oh on this set
> You've been begging and dying for somebody's rhyming
>   to set you free
> For God so loved the world he gave to me
> I'm cooling, teacher knows me in school and
> The mic, this mic in my hand, I'm ruling
> So prepare your mind for my lifeline
> And meet the new Queen of Royal Badness
> Latifah has the spirit so head for the water
> And dive into the wrath of my madness
>   [First verse of "Wrath of My Madness"]

The demo went from Mark to Fab Five Freddy, a video jockey and phenomenon on *Yo! MTV Raps*. Riding the surge in popularity of rap music and rap culture, the station was waking up to the money to be made from white and African-American audiences.

Fab Five Freddy liked the demo so much that he sent it to Tommy Boy Records. Monica Lynch, the head of artist development, phoned Latifah only days later to talk about a record deal. Thus six months after her high school graduation, Queen Latifah was signed: "Success is when opportunity meets preparation. All I needed was the opportunity."

Building on what she had seen and heard in New York clubs and at basement rap parties, Latifah began to forge her own style of rap, putting everything she had into her music.

Her career was off to a running start, and Latifah credits her friend Ramsey for his encouragement and for his unique friendship, the standard to which Latifah now holds all her friends and which she has also set for herself:

> It's rare to have friends who want more for you than you do for yourself. . . . But Ramsey wanted to see us all succeed. And he was willing to make sacrifices. He risked getting evicted. He ate mayonnaise sandwiches for weeks. He would do almost anything to find the money for us to get studio time so that we could perfect our demos.
>
> Ramsey saw Queen Latifah even before I did. He was a seer—and a magician. Not just for the vision he had for all of us, but for the way he held our group together.

Latifah's first album, *All Hail the Queen*, was released in 1989 to widespread acclaim, receiving a Grammy nomination, reaching the top 10 on *Billboard*'s R&B chart, and going platinum. The album included the singles from her demo and "Ladies First," a song she recorded as a duet with Monie Love. The combination of rap, R&B, reggae, and dance music, along with thoughtful lyrics, was successful with critics and fans alike and in 1990 she was voted Best Female Rapper by *Rolling Stone* readers. The New Music Seminar in New York, the biggest convention in the business, named her the Best New Artist of 1990. "Ladies First" was later to be included in the Rock 'N' Roll Hall Of Fame's 500 Songs That Shaped Rock And Roll.

In *All Hail the Queen*, Latifah gave voice to the rising frustration among many black women, expressing her anger at black male rappers for their attitude towards women. She has never tried to play herself as being in opposition to male rappers, however. On the contrary, Latifah has repeatedly refused to criticize her fellow rappers directly, but rather to promote a dialogue through her music. Dialogue in music is a constant—musicians engage in discourse even if they are not doing it consciously. In their communicating and reacting to their history, their fans, and their fellow musicians, new music develops.

Queen Latifah has taken part in a conscious dialogue, which often gives her lyrics more depth and weight. Rappers such as Public Enemy and Ice-T take part in a broader dialogue about race and society, speaking to those in authority and to the dynamics of our culture—giving their lyrics the added weight of controversy. In "Ladies First," Latifah enters the dialogue to reaffirm the African-American woman's place in her people's history, and the potential for her role in the future. Her focus on her heritage influenced her rap handle "Queen," as homage to the fact that black men and women come from a long line of kings and queens ignored. She does not attack black men nor even refer to them in the song. She samples the voice of Malcolm X throughout as a way to reinforce black women's contributions to the liberation of black people everywhere.

Preparing for her first promotional pictures, Tommy Boy gave her money to buy new clothes, but Latifah did not want to look like everyone else—she wanted to have her own style. She went to an African clothing store and had the owner help her fashion an outfit made with African patterns; she also created a "crown" from the same material in the fashion of a traditional African headpiece. Finding no shoes that matched, Latifah went barefoot to the photo shoot. She had defined her own style, and she would wear it throughout her first tour.

In 1989, Latifah was also part of a rap collective called the Native Tongues, which included Monie Love, De La Soul, and A Tribe Called Quest as part

As rap evolved, artists like Public Enemy and Ice-T (seen here during a TV appearance) began to fuel their lyrics with their often controversial views on race and society. These artists spurred Latifah to write powerful songs about the pride and heritage of black women.

of the group, with the Jungle Brothers as the head-liners. The focus of the collective was to promote African history among African Americans, thereby promoting unity. This was part of an emerging trend in the world of hip-hop and rap that the success of Public Enemy helped impel—an Afro-centric worldview that was a source of strength and inspiration to many.

It was the positive influence of people like Professor Griff of Public Enemy and her friend Shakim, now her business partner, that helped her navigate through a world often hostile to women. Frequently duped by promoters during this time, female rappers constantly had to be careful about money issues, a parallel with the difficulties women generally were facing in society. Shakim became her road manager, the one she could trust to watch out for her and make sure she got paid.

Her second album followed closely on the heels of the first's success. She had toured Europe and Japan already, had been given the Best New Artist Award in 1990 by the New Music Seminar of Manhattan, and had made a guest TV appearance on Will Smith's *The Fresh Prince of Bel-Air*. The album *Nature of a Sista*, released in 1991, continued her fast climb to fame. Other television appearances ensued, as well as a bit part in Spike Lee's movie *Jungle Fever*. She had already begun investing in small businesses in her native Newark, showing that she was a woman of power and substance in all aspects of her life.

She was riding high, and her family and friends were extremely proud. Speaking of her influences in an *Essence* interview, Latifah is clear:

> It really took the whole village with me. Everywhere I go, I pick up something from someone, and what I can't use, I leave by the wayside. My father's side of the family is real street-smart. Not in a Fortune 500 kind of thing, but entrepreneurs. They do whatever has to be done. My mom's side of the family had a very wholesome upbringing. That blending gave me a real strong foundation. My friends helped raise me in a lot

While working on her music, Latifah also began to show her talents in films. Here she is in a scene from House Party 2.

of ways, too. We all kind of guided each other because we all had dreams and wanted to be somebody. We weren't just ghetto kids filled with hopelessness. Your family and how you're raised is very important because you can lose yourself in the entertainment business, in anything involving money.

She would need this support and love more than she could guess in the years that followed. When tragedy strikes, how one handles it matters most in the long run.

4

REIGN OF DARKNESS

❧

QUEEN LATIFAH HAD bought a house in Wayne, New Jersey—a shell of a house that she could design as she wanted it. In 1992, while bouncing back and forth between Europe, record-label appointments, and promotional gigs, Latifah was missing her family. She had moved out at 18 years old, but was ready to have her family under one roof again. She also had a goal. More than becoming a famous rapper, she wanted to be able to repay her mother and brother for always being there. She wanted to make sure they never lacked anything, and her financial success was making that goal become a reality.

The house was one of five on the block, and had enough room so that she, her brother, and her mother could have their own space. Woods enclosing the backyard and the skylights and large deck were added bonuses. Visions of a full house, friends and family celebrating life together, filled her head. A night or so after she closed on the house, she and Winki explored it with only his police flashlight to guide them. One month had passed from that night, and 24-year-old Winki was dead.

Seeing her brother in his police uniform, laid out in his silver coffin, Latifah was in a daze. The number of people who came out to say good-bye to her brother was comforting, but it would be a long time and a lot of grief before she could see the other side of this

After her brother's death, Latifah found she could channel her sadness and rage through her music.

heartbreak. The questions that bombard the psyche after a tragic loss such as this one can drive a person to despair, and Latifah struggled with these feelings and more after her brother's death.

The relationship the two shared went deeper than just sister and brother. Lancelot Owens Jr. was her dearest companion as a child, her protector, and the man of the house after their parents split up. His humor and wit, his cheerful outlook on life, and his commitment to his family were just some of the ways in which he inspired his little sister. At 22 years old, few sisters would plan to have a brother live with them:

> Winki was one of my best friends, but not because he was my brother. I know plenty of people who can't stand their brothers or their sisters, and that's a real shame. Blood doesn't necessarily mean connection or love or friendship. Even family relationships require work. . . . You have to let everyone. . . know how much they mean to you—with hugs, words of encouragement, and spending time together.
>
> Winki and I did that all our lives.

Blaming God was Latifah's first reaction. Winki was planning to marry his girlfriend and had received numerous commendations from the Newark police force, and Latifah understandably felt that it was unfair for God to take him away. Her rage and grief poured out of her daily. She often wondered why she had not been taken instead. She would gladly have given her own life to spare her brother's.

Her friend Tammy, a close friend since childhood, helped her through much of this time by refusing to allow Latifah to give up or to place blame on God. Tammy's mother, whom Latifah also loved and thought of as her second mother, had died three years before. Her death had given Tammy authority that compelled Latifah to listen. One night in Tammy's room, with Stevie Wonder in the background,

Tammy sat by as Latifah in her sorrow kicked and screamed and hit the walls, over and over, then exhausted, fell sobbing to the floor. When she became still, Tammy softly spoke to her of the Bible and what others had endured—reassuring her that she would, too. She told her to think about Winki in Heaven; she had no doubt that that was where he was, and if Latifah could listen, she would hear him speaking to her, offering her comfort.

Latifah describes losing a loved one as similar to losing a limb. The pain remains long after the arm or leg is gone—there is a constant itching sensation reminding one of what is lost. She knew Winki could never be completely gone, though, because the body is merely a shell housing our spirits temporarily. Without these beliefs sustaining her, Latifah believes that she might have ended her own life, so great was the pain.

Latifah and her mother grieved in very different ways. Unable to face the reality, Latifah turned to marijuana, alcohol, and basketball, going through the motions of her day while hiding behind blue sunglasses. Holding everything in, Rita just would not let herself cry—at least not in front of her daughter. Yet they supported each other in a constant intuitive awareness of the other's suffering. Separated by Latifah's work in California, they were to find a kind of solace independently. Latifah was able to accept a doctor in California who encouraged her to talk through her rage, and Rita found some peace through her art.

Her father broke down from the guilt of all the years he had missed. After the accident he came to Rita's house and sat in the kitchen crying, saying over and over again how they had taken his "chicken," his pet name for his son whom he kept "under his wing." As a father, he could not understand why his son was gone when he himself had been close to death in war and as a police officer so many times, yet was still alive. Eventually, he reached inside far enough to know that he had to have help, which he soon sought.

For Latifah, drinking and smoking pot was all she could do to get through any given day, but eventually her brother himself seemed to bring her the spirit that she needed, as he would continue to do many times through her sorrow.

Looming before her was an agreement with Motown to finish her third album. She could not find the strength to complete it. But she recalled how her brother had always taught her to face pain head-on, never to run away. Working on the songs she and her brother had shared would perhaps help her to stay close to him. She would channel her rage and sadness into productiveness.

> But I never shut up when things piss me off
> And if I got to curse at you to get my point across
> That's what I got to do, that's how it's got to be
> I've got an angel watchin' over me.
> —From "Winki's Theme"

She poured herself into the album with everything she had—as if her very life depended on it—and it was a matter of survival, ultimately. "I had to free my soul by releasing the pain through my music. It found an escape."

Black Reign was released in 1993, an album as much her brother's as hers, and a monument not only to her own strength but to the remarkable bond between brother and sister. She chose for the cover of the album a photograph of herself at Winki's grave, as tribute to him. Written across the picture are the words, "I Love U & Miss U more than words could ever express."

Reviews were positive. The critics hailed her powerful voice and her use of a wide variety of influences on the album: "She is probably hip hop's most assured and exciting female performer" and "[Latifah]

Queen Latifah
Black Reign

The album Black Reign, *released in 1993, showed a new power in her lyrics. The album is as much a monument to Latifah's personal strength as a memorial to her brother. As the cover photo, Latifah chose a photo of herself at her brother's grave.*

is at her best when she goes hardcore and unleashes the skills and attitude that made her famous" were some of the things being said.

The songs range from the hardcore sounds of "Rough" and "Bring the Flavor," with guests such as KRS-1 and Heavy D helping her out, to an R&B-style duet with Tony Rebel; from dance party jams to the unique anthem for her brother, "Winki's Theme," which combines several jazz and hip-hop styles. Then there is the single that won her the Grammy Award in 1994 for Best Rap Solo Performance, "U.N.I.T.Y." —a salute to women that details the disrespect she has witnessed by black men toward women, specifically influenced by observing behavior at a Greek Picnic in Philadelphia, Pennsylvania.

A Greek Picnic is a gathering of African-American fraternities and sororities from colleges all over the nation as a way to network and share strength with one another, but Latifah was dismayed when she saw how some men mistreated the women. The song became an anthem for many black women:

> Instinct leads me to another flow
> Everytime I hear a brother call a girl a ***** or a ho
> Trying to make a sister feel low
> You know all of that gots to go
> Now everybody knows there's exceptions to this rule
> Now don't be getting mad, when we playing, it's cool
> But don't you be calling out my name
> I bring wrath to those who disrespect me like a dame

There was surprise by some at the amount of singing, as opposed to rapping, that appeared on the album. For Latifah, however, it is not about making a separation between hip-hop and R&B. Her singing comes from her heart, and the music needs to fit. For Latifah, there is no one style big enough to hold her. Ask her and she will call it "flavor" that makes her music different. The flavor means special, and her music is that. The album became her biggest seller, eventually making her the first female rap artist to hit gold and giving her far more exposure on radio and MTV than she had previously had.

Soon after the release of *Black Reign*, Latifah landed her role in *Living Single*, which required that she move to Los Angeles. Her acting career had become important in her life, giving her the opportunity to work in films (*House Party 2* and *Juice*) with actors such as Tupac Shakur, Samuel L. Jackson, and Omar Epps. Although her role in *Juice* was small, the movie explored issues of interest to her—the violence in the ghetto and the black man's position that violence is equal to credibility.

Latifah had already established Flavor Unit Entertainment with her friend Shakim Compere, an enterprise aimed at recognizing and nurturing the talent in others. She and Shakim serve as copresidents, with Latifah's mother as vice president. The business includes a record label, film and television production

companies, an artist management company, and, most recently, a real estate company. Flavor Unit manages such groups as Naughty by Nature, L.L. Cool J., and Monica. In honor of her brother and also to continue with her desire to give back to her community, Latifah and her mother established the Lancelot H. Owens Foundation in 1993, an organization that gives scholarships to students with exceptional scholastic ability and limited financial means.

These endeavors, running out to L.A. to star in a sitcom, creating her own business, and taking roles in the major motion pictures in which she had so far

With roles in movies like Juice, *Latifah showed she had talent in front of a camera as well as a microphone.*

appeared, however, left Latifah still feeling empty. Recovering from a tragedy is rather like one step forward and two steps backward. Her brother was not there to share in her continued success, and while she pushed onward, her feelings of guilt, of despair, and of sorrow were always fighting against her forward movement:

> I wasn't moving, progressing. I was making movies, television shows, records, but inside, I was stunted. My relationships could only get so deep, because there was no room for another person. The memory of Winki took up most of the space in my heart.

Later Queen Latifah would recognize that when she saw Winki's mangled motorcycle in the hospital parking lot, she began to tap into an inner strength of which she was unaware. She would also see that her ability to move through life, even with the intense sorrow, was a gift. That she could finish the album, that she could move out to L.A. and work hard on her television show—that took strength. But initially her emotional energies had been caught up in wondering why it happened and how she could get over it, rather than how to move through it with God. The psychiatrist had helped. A stigma exists in the African-American community against going to such doctors, but her need for help was more important. She prayed and went to church, she spoke with friends and relatives, but eventually she understood that it was time she needed the most.

Before she could fully grasp these lessons, other difficulties would contribute to her emotional turmoil and further stretch her long time of recovery. In July of 1995, while her career continued to grow, a frightening and horrible incident occurred. In Harlem with her bodyguard Sean Moon, Latifah in the driver's seat, Sean on the passenger side, two armed carjackers approached them while the car was stopped. They ordered Latifah out of the car and shot Sean

In 1996, Latifah faced another tragedy—an armed carjacking and the near-fatal shooting of friend and bodyguard Sean Moon. Here, she enters the courthouse to testify at the trial of one of the carjackers.

in the stomach. Her fortunate ability to react calmly probably saved his life, according to police reports. Without hesitating, she dashed into the traffic to flag down a car to get Moon to the hospital.

In the aftermath of this shock on top of her brother's death, Latifah unfortunately went back to what she felt would get her through the day-to-day activities of life. Motivated by fear and anguish, she was carrying a gun and marijuana when the police stopped her in 1996 for speeding. By all accounts, Latifah seems to have been relieved to be stopped in her tracks. The officer at the scene was quoted as saying that she was honest and straight-forward in response to his questions, readily admitting to having the gun and pot in the car. What makes this attitude more incredible is that Latifah had already had the experience of being stopped by police for no reason—other than being a black woman in an expensive BMW. She had had officers ask her what she was "doing in such an expensive car," and had been made to explain herself and her money and her ability to pay for it. While these incidents had been upsetting to her, they did not make her disrespectful to the officer who stopped her this time. Her willingness to plead guilty to the charges and to face up to her wrongs illustrates well her true character.

Her punishment consisted of a fine of $810 and a donation of $2,500 to a charity for disadvantaged youth in Los Angeles, as well as a two-year probation, a ban on owning or holding any weapons, and the destruction of the gun with which she was caught. The punishment turned out to be a gift, in retrospect, because it marked a new beginning for the Queen. There have been no such incidents since, and her focus on nurturing the royalty in others has been unwavering in its determination.

In an interview in 1999, when asked about feeling lost because of the loss of her brother, Latifah's positive attitude shines with the wisdom that comes from making it through hard times:

> But the road back is the most fun part, you know. Because there is a road back from all of that stuff. And when you find it, it's like a light that just shines on you. And then you start taking this walk. You don't know what's coming, but you're not afraid of it, you know. Which makes it more exciting than just being unhappy, and being alone and being afraid.

Today she can let go of Winki without letting it mean forgetting. Latifah feels her brother's presence

The all-female Lilith Fair gave Latifah another opportunity to show her talents. Appearing with other women artists and singer-songwriters like Sheryl Crow and the Dixie Chicks, she performed to packed arenas around the country.

and support, and always will feel that love. Today, her faith in God and her honoring of her inner strength and beauty are what keep her grounded through continued success. The darkness had begun to lift, and Queen Latifah aimed to be a living example of what can happen if one does not give up.

5

INTO THE LIGHT

❧

QUEEN LATIFAH THE actress began to come to the forefront in the role of Khadijah on *Living Single*. She also created the show's theme music. *Living Single* aired on the Fox network from 1993 to 1998; the five-year run allowed the positive role model that Latifah portrayed to enter the thought and actions of the African-American mainstream. The show was so successful that when it was to end in 1997, a massive African-American letter-writing campaign delayed its cancellation, enabling *Living Single* to run through 1998. The character Khadijah James was very like Latifah herself—a strong, independent woman who founded her own magazine *Flavor*, which was a medium for women's perspective as Latifah created her company Flavor to support the efforts of her black musician friends. Flavor, of course, had been part of the name of Latifah's early rapper group, the Flavor Unit. In the 1990s and under Latifah's guidance, it would become Flavor Unit Management, designed to support and manage rappers' careers. It rapidly evolved into a management company representing artists outside their group. Flavor Unit began in 1995 to record Latifah's artists as well as managing their engagements. In 1996, the company expanded again with a West Coast office. Ironically enough, however, as Flavor

Putting African-American women in the spotlight as strong, positive characters was a big part of the success enjoyed by the TV show Living Single. *Latifah not only acted in the show, she created its music as well. Here's the cast in a publicity photo.*

Unit Entertainment grew, *Living Single* ceased to continue to develop.

The sitcom takes place in New York City where three of the characters—Khadijah, her cousin, and a childhood friend—live together in a brownstone. Rounding out the group is Maxine, a public defender and Khadijah's best friend, who spends most of her time at the apartment. For tension and romance, there are the two men from upstairs, one who is the boyfriend to Khadijah's cousin, and the other who has the classic love-hate relationship with Maxine.

The intense schedule of filming a sitcom was good for Latifah during this adjustment period of her life, keeping her busy. Her best friend Tammy came out to stay with her during the first season to help keep her focused and took on the role of physical trainer when Latifah asked. Coming home from a full day of shooting and having Tammy command her to get ready to exercise made Latifah second-guess her decision, but she knew that on her own she would not have the discipline.

Latifah was making films simultaneously with her TV acting. One film in particular would showcase her talent. Though in 1993 she played opposite Michael Keaton in *My Life*, it was her role as Cleo in the 1996 action movie *Set It Off* that made reviewers begin to take notice. The movie, director F. Gary Gray's second film, has been described as *Waiting to Exhale* with guns. It also has been compared to *Thelma and Louise* and *Dead Presidents*. As one reviewer wrote, "The concept of four black action heroines makes for a welcome change in a genre that is dominated by: (a) rugged white males with a perpetual five o'clock shadow, (b) rugged white males who speak English with an accent, and (c) rugged white males with the acting ability of a fence post."

In the film My Life, Latifah played opposite star Michael Keaton. During this time, she was working on TV and in the recording studio.

The plot revolves around four friends, one of whom works as a teller in a bank. The first half-hour shows Frankie (played by Vivica A. Fox) at work while the bank is being robbed. Recognizing one of the robbers from her neighborhood, she calls out to him. In the aftermath, Frankie is grilled by police and summarily fired by her white boss. Angry and embittered, she vents to her friends. When word gets out that Darnell, the one Frankie knew, made off with $20,000, the women start wondering if maybe they, too, could rob a bank.

But the film is not as predictable as one might think, and that is what surprised many reviewers. The sensitivity to the economic issues involved with these four women is well portrayed. The financial troubles are not used to justify their behavior or to assert that robbing a bank is okay, but rather to give the characters a depth rarely found in others of this particular film genre. Roger Ebert of the *Chicago Sun-Times* wrote, "The movie surprised and moved me: I expected a routine action picture and was amazed how much I cared about the characters." In 1997 Latifah won the Best Actress award at the Black Film Awards and a Best Supporting Actress award from the Independent Film Awards for her role.

The film spurred gang violence, however, much to her dismay, with incidents occurring in New York, Washington, D.C., and southern California. Even two years later, in August of 1998, five females were arrested after robbing a bank in Olympia, Washington. These women played out the movie complete with three entering the bank in hooded sweatshirts, dark stocking caps, and bandanas while one stayed outside to stand guard. They counted off the clock, completing the robbery in fifty-three seconds, and then thanked the tellers and customers before fleeing on foot. When police caught the women in their shared home, they found a copy of *Set It Off*. Latifah has made it clear in interviews that people were getting the wrong message from the movie—it was not meant to promote violence but rather to show that the characters had made the wrong choices.

Some segment of any audience will always take in only the most literal meaning of a film. This segment would be those who interpreted the film

as promoting violence and who just as blindly failed to distinguish between the actress Latifah and the role of Cleo in *Set It Off*, setting abroad rumors about Latifah's sexuality. Reactions from critics and fans ranged from shock to awe at her acting abilities in the character of Cleo, a strong and loud lesbian who wants the money to buy things for her girlfriend.

For Latifah, the role was a challenge that she welcomed as a test of her acting ability, a way to stretch herself as an actress. Only by performing a

Latifah's first major critical acclaim for her acting came with the 1996 release of Set It Off, *a movie featuring four black women in powerful, action-filled roles. Here she is in a still from the film, with costars Vivica Fox, Kimberly Elise, and Jada Pinkett.*

role that was opposite to her true nature would she be capable of measuring her talent:

> Hey, that's the role. I'm an actor. I didn't really have a choice in defining the character's sexuality. . . . I'm hired to make Cleo a real person in your minds. Cleo is gay and I can't change her because of people's mindsets in America. It would be a lot easier on me if I could because I wouldn't have to deal with questions like this and any controversy that may come. But I'm an actor. I can't show you the talent that I have and the skills that I have by playing Queen Latifah all over again 80 times in another movie. . . . I wanted to do something completely different.

She thus has for the most part ignored questions and rumors about her sexuality since they do not apply to Latifah the woman. Her acting career remains a focal point in her life. As well as her involvement in acting, she has the courage of her convictions in her professional and her personal life. She will go to a gay club or a straight club depending on how she feels, and she refuses to worry about reactions.

She knows well that people often rush to judgments based on ridiculous standards, not only skin color, but speech patterns and accents, clothing styles, haircuts, and the kind of car a person drives. All become bases for erroneous and sometimes cruel judgments. The concept of a strong, independent-thinking, intelligent woman doesn't fit a small societal group's need for women to be weak so that it can appear strong.

> It's insulting when someone asks, "Are you gay?" A woman cannot be strong, outspoken, competent at running her own business, handle herself physically, play a very convincing role in a movie, know what she wants—and go for it—without being gay? Come on.

While she knew others thought she should go right out for a boyfriend to counter all the gossip, she held firm and refused to let the malicious few dictate her behavior. She had never gotten involved with a man purely for other people's benefit, and she was not about to now simply because of a foolish rumor.

Latifah has had many relationships over the years, some of which were mistakes from the start, and some of which developed into lasting friendships. Mondo, whom she met when she was only 14 years old, is a man she holds up as keeping her faith in men. He treated her with respect and helped her overcome shame over her body image, and she is grateful for that.

Another positive example she mentions in her autobiography is Ferric Collons, a defensive end for the Raiders football team when they met. They had much in common, and she respected him for not being intimidated by her. As a strong woman, she continues to encounter men whom she intimidates; Collons was a welcome change. The relationship grew out of a mutual appreciation of their differences and enjoyment of shared interests. They agreed to end it when their careers began to happen on opposite coasts and schedules, but they continue to see each other, although on an infrequent basis.

Latifah knows that men are rarely more perfect than women, and that the opposite is also true. As a consequence, she refuses to bash men as "dogs":

> I give every man in my life the benefit of the doubt. They come into the situation with a free pass, a complete pie. If they choose to eat away at that pie by lying and cheating and doing stupid things, that's on them. Once they eat half, I take my half and I'm gone. I don't wait around for them to eat my half, too.

When asked why the "Queen" in front of her name, Latifah usually answers that it was because she did not want to be "MC Latifah." She did not want to be just another MC in the ever-growing sea of rap music. The title has taken on deeper meaning through the years, however. She does not keep the name to portray herself as "better-than," but rather, to celebrate her strength and to encourage others to do the same. She uses it as an affirmation —if one thinks of oneself with respect, then one commands respect from others.

Rather than seeing men as villains, she sees black men as victims. One of her goals is to start a school specifically geared to the needs of African-American boys, whom she sees as needing special nurturing. In an interview, when speaking of the violent death of Tupac Shakur and male love, Latifah had this to say:

> Everybody wants male love. Guys like Tupac seek it in their companions, their homies, in their fathers. And they're going to seek it in other places if they don't get it from their fathers. Women are going to seek male love, too. They're going to seek it whether the man is right or wrong for them. People are starving for male love because it hasn't been there consistently over the past couple hundred years, at least not in Black America. It's something we crave so bad that we do all kinds of crazy things to get it. I know that it doesn't matter how many child-support payments my father missed along the way, when I see him, I love him, regardless.

Her portrayal of Cleo in *Set It Off* marked a new beginning for the Queen. A year later she won the Aretha Franklin Award for Entertainer of the Year at the Soul Train Lady of Soul Awards. Her persistence, her patience, and her willingness to take responsibility for her own actions were finally paying off, and she had found as well a greater sense of peace through

having been understood and appreciated by the entertainment industry.

Taking time alone has become an important tool in her life to learn how to be happy with who she is. Her favorite ways to be alone are to take a long, hot bath with music playing, or to go out to the beach early in the morning or into the woods when no one else is around. She now makes a habit of taking that time out from daily life to contemplate where she is, where she is going, and if she is

Latifah has stayed clear of the violence that has claimed the lives of so many male rappers like Tupac Shakur, pictured here in a scene from the film Poetic Justice.

In 1997, the Queen received the Aretha Franklin Award for Entertainer of the Year at the Soul Train Lady of Soul Awards.

being true to the queen she knows herself to be.

Her real strength lies in that introspection and her faith in God. Seeing herself through the eyes of God and the eyes of her mother, Latifah finds it easier to check herself and to recognize when a behavior needs changing. She does not beat herself up, however—the idea is not to berate oneself for poor behavior, but to align oneself more closely with the way in which God (or whatever one's concept of God is) would have a person live. Focusing on the fact that we are all made in the image of God, Latifah can trust that God would not want her to treat herself badly or allow anyone else to do so.

That has become the main message of Queen Latifah, and one she proudly declares. It is this attitude, one that was there all along but needed some time along the way in order for her to wear it comfortably, that has been behind her ongoing accomplishments.

6

QUEEN OF ALL
SHE SURVEYS

T HE YEAR 1998 was another banner year for Queen Latifah. Her long-awaited fourth album, *Order in the Court*, was finally released and her acting career continued to grow. In the television miniseries *Mama Flora's Family*, based on a book by Alex Haley, she played the niece of the family matriarch. A hip-hop remake of *The Wizard of Oz* also aired with rappers Snoop Doggy Dogg and Heavy D, in which she portrayed the Wicked Witch of the West. She appeared in the mainstream movie *Sphere* with Dustin Hoffman, Samuel L. Jackson, and Sharon Stone—a movie that critics did not particularly like, but no one found fault with Latifah's performance.

Order in the Court, while not receiving the raves that her previous releases had, was still well received. *The Source* wrote, "With the wrath of her musical madness, this fiery lady was determined to uplift the state of female rappers still stranded in the aural wasteland of the post-Roxanne era." *Entertainment Weekly* wrote, "On her latest album, the multimedia maven splits the difference between thumping hip-hop and suave lover-girl R&B jams, all the while reminding her royal subjects exactly who reigns supreme. With an album this fun and funky, it's hard to argue with her."

The songs range in style, as has been typical of her previous albums, and the lyrics and messages

Latifah publicizes the 1998 release of her fourth album, Order in the Court, *on her own record label, Flavor Unit.*

continue to be profound. She describes the album as being about her thoughts concerning love, life, God, and music, which covers just about everything that really matters. In "What You Gonna Do," Latifah sings of the grief she will always feel over her brother's death. There is the harder-edged single "Bananas," the smooth-sounding "Paper," and then there are the jazz-influenced songs, such as "Black on Black Love," which addresses the importance of African Americans caring for one another, and "Life," a song in honor of Tupac Shakur and Notorious B.I.G., both of whom were shot and killed at the beginning of their career. Speaking about the album's delay to MTV, Latifah said this:

> A lot of queens came along while I was away from my throne for a moment . . . and it's all good. I don't knock anybody, but I'm holding my spot. . . . The thing about me is that I've never competed with anyone else because I've always done my own thing. So in my mind, I'm not in competition with any other female rappers out there. No other female rapper can make Latifah records, just like I can't make Foxy records, I can't make Kim records. . . . But this is what I'll do, I'll assert myself in my own way, and I'll hold my throne like I always do.

Her performance in 1998's *Living Out Loud*, however, brought her the most attention that year. Starring Academy Award winner Holly Hunter and Danny DeVito, it was Queen Latifah who stole the show. Her strong, sultry voice as Liz Bailey the jazz singer came as a thrilling surprise to critics and fans who knew her only as a rap artist. The soundtrack has become a hit with jazz fans overall. Latifah herself considered it her best work since *Set It Off*.

Inspired by two Anton Chekhov short stories, the movie explores themes of loneliness, life lessons, and human connections. Judith Nelson is the wife of a wealthy doctor, living on Fifth Avenue in New York

City. When her husband leaves her for a younger woman, she is left to ponder her life and her unfulfilled dreams. A chance encounter with a stranger who mistakes her for another woman and kisses her in the dark awakens her sexuality and faith in humanity. She ends up befriending the elevator operator Pat (DeVito), who she discovers also has hopes and dreams beyond what she perceived. His wife has tossed him out because of his gambling, and he struggles with his need to feel independent and the impending loss of his dying daughter. Liz Bailey, played by Queen Latifah, is a singer in a local lounge who becomes the friend and confidant of the two characters.

In an interview with Byron Allen on *Entertainers*, Latifah describes Liz and the other characters as being people going through changes, trying to find some peace. She views the movie as being about the bad relationships people find themselves in, wondering why they are with someone who does not really know them, and then learning to discover their individual joys—discovering life.

In her role as the lounge singer, Latifah sings such jazz and blues standards as Billy Strayhorn's "Lush Life," Irving Gordon's "Be Anything (But Be Mine)," and Little Anthony and the Imperials' "Goin' Out of My Head." Her vocal range impressed and amazed anyone who listened, including writer and director Richard LaGravenese, whose screenplays include *The Horse Whisperer*, *The Fisher King*, and *Beloved*, and music producer Mervyn Warren.

Warren traveled to New York to rehearse with Latifah to quell his fears about her ability to sing in this different genre. In performing his arrangement of "Lush Life," Warren worried that she would not be able to manage what many considered to be one of the most difficult songs to perform. "The truth is," he said, "she just nailed it."

In fact, LaGravenese originally had in mind a

40-year-old to play the role of Liz Bailey the torch singer. When Latifah expressed interest in the part and the two met, however, he was thoroughly impressed by the star's motivation to sing the songs and decided on her for the part. When he heard what she and Mervyn Warren accomplished with "Lush Life," he realized that he had made an even better decision than he had thought.

Dana Owens grew up listening to jazz and blues artists, such as Sarah Vaughan and Ella Fitzgerald, whom her parents loved. So she too knew and loved the songs for the *Living Out Loud* soundtrack. The results of her hard work and her obvious and natural singing talent brought the movie to life. As Roger Ebert said in his review, "Queen Latifah shows here (as she did in *Set It Off*) that her screen presence makes a scene stand up and hum. Anyone who can steal a scene from Danny DeVito and Holly Hunter can do just about anything in a movie."

DeVito and Hunter were equally impressed by Latifah's performance, and both praised her abilities in interviews. For Latifah, though, taking on the role was part and parcel of her desire to push the boundaries of what she had done previously—not to allow herself to be defined by those boundaries. She had reached a point in her life and her career where fear no longer held a place. She had no doubts as to her ability to perform the role of Liz Bailey, and to perform it extremely well. Her reasoning behind wanting to play the part in the first place speaks to her ever-emerging sense of responsibility to play roles in movies that she feels are important roles.

She sees honor in remaining true to herself by taking on challenges and not allowing herself to be stereotyped. After the release of *Living Out Loud*, she wrapped up the filming of *The Bone Collector*, starring Denzel Washington and Angelina Jolie. She plays a nurse, Thelma, who cares for Washington's character, a quadriplegic police officer helping to hunt a

serial killer. Jolie replaces his mobility with hers and takes in all that his eyes and ears would if he were not incapacitated.

She credits Denzel with teaching her much more about acting. On the set, he answered questions she had been hesitant to ask before. He gave her advice and showed her by example that there are no stupid questions, only stupid answers. And once again, she

The same year as her Order in the Court *CD hit the record stores, Latifah starred in* Living Out Loud, *in which she played a jazz singer opposite stars Holly Hunter and Danny DeVito.*

had the experience of appearing in a movie that did not fare well with the critics, but one in which her performance drew acclaim.

Latifah is very aware that there are few roles available to black women, and that they often must compete for the same roles. She also tries to avoid roles that can be played only by black women. She trusts her intuition above all when deciding on a role. If her instincts tell her she should do it because it will be worth the work, then she accepts it.

Fueled by the successes of that year, Latifah looked forward, keeping her eyes on the many goals she has set for herself. She began negotiations with William Morrow and Company to write an inspirational autobiography. Published in 1999, *Ladies First: Revelations of a Strong Woman*, with Karen Hunter, a *New York Daily News* reporter, brought further recognition for Latifah as a woman of many talents. In the book, Latifah aims to encourage and support not only black women, but all women and men in their daily lives by sharing her own experiences.

Dedicated "to every woman who has ever felt like less than royalty," the book explores issues of self-esteem with a gut-level honesty and candor that reviewers praised. Different from a straight autobiography in that it does not give a direct chronological account, and different from a self-help book in that it does not preach, *Ladies First* enables Latifah to reach out to many young women who are struggling in their own lives, and she gives them hope.

Much of it is written in the style of speech, and the effect is one of sitting down to chat with Dana Owens, the real person. Her frank and open attitude about her own difficulties with drugs, with sex, and with the grief of losing her brother makes her strength very apparent, her struggles even more impressive.

In her introduction she gives the disclaimer that

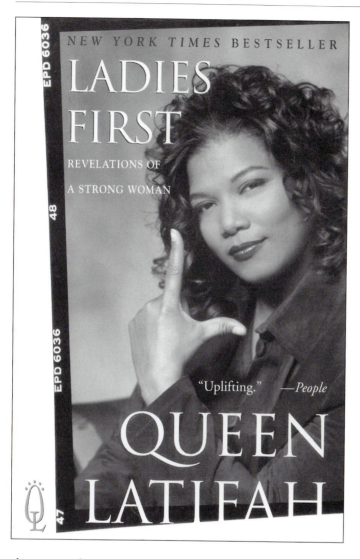

NEW YORK TIMES BESTSELLER

LADIES FIRST

REVELATIONS OF

A STRONG WOMAN

EPD 6036

48

EPD 6036

"Uplifting."   —*People*

QUEEN LATIFAH

47

Always eager to emphasize the strength of black women, Latifah put her own experiences to paper in the book Ladies First.

she is neither a psychologist nor an expert on life, but it is this approach that gives her words more weight. It is the same reason one alcoholic helping another alcoholic works—the painful times have been experienced by both, and therefore one is more willing to listen. Latifah's personal experience lends genuine authority to her voice. Her ability to overcome obstacles gives hope to those women whose difficult lives have impaired or destroyed their self-esteem and confidence.

As Queen of the Coney Island Mermaid Parade, Latifah shows off her style.

Her wish, as expressed in her introduction, is for women to recognize themselves as being worthy of the title queen. She mentions women such as Jackie Kennedy Onassis and Betty Shabazz, the wife of Malcolm X, as examples of queens—women who held their heads high in the face of adversity and pain. She honors her mother, Rita Owens, as being the one to lay the foundation, showing her by example how to be a self-proclaimed queen.

"Queenliness," Latifah writes, "is an attitude that starts on the inside and works its way out."

Her attitude is one of inner power—that by projecting oneself as a queen one will be treated as such. She stresses pride in one's work no matter what type of work it is, and treating oneself and others with respect. Because she always remembers that she is a child of God, as are we all, no shame can dethrone her or anyone else: "I know who I am. I am confident. I know God. I can take care of myself. I share my life with others, and I love—I am worthy of the title Queen. So are you."

That focus has sustained her through many difficulties, and today she has no difficulty holding her head high, and with good reason.

7

WE ARE ALL ROYALTY

‧‧

As IF HER large company, her many motion picture roles, her last album, and her well-received autobiography were not keeping her busy enough, Queen Latifah also began preproduction talks in 1998 about a syndicated talk show. Friend Rosie O'Donnell, who had been enjoying great success with her own talk show, was the one to remark that Latifah would be a great host. She recognized Latifah's humor and abilities and now serves as a consultant on *The Queen Latifah Show*. Latifah's good friend and business partner, Shakim Compere, also encouraged her and became one of the coproducers.

Debuting in September of 1999, the show has run for three seasons. Continuing her visions of helping to improve the world around her, Latifah uses her show as a way to encourage the same values in others that she herself has emulated. The show's success comes from her appeal to a diverse audience. The topics generally concern standard issues, such as teen pregnancy and finding lost loves, but she also combines musical entertainment and has famous guests give advice on personal issues. Once, for example, she had Snoop Dogg as a guest when the focus was on urging kids to get out of gangs.

Some of the people who have appeared on her show include Whoopi Goldberg, Ice Cube, Brooke Shields, and Al Gore. During her interview with

Combining current issues and musical entertainment, The Queen Latifah Show burst onto the talk show scene in 1999. Here she interviews presidential candidate Al Gore.

Gore, Latifah asked questions that were different from the usual routine to which the candidate was accustomed, and his candid responses surprised many in the invited student audience. He shared family photos, spoke about playing drinking games in college, and told stories about his motorcycle-riding days. In addition to quizzing the vice president about pop culture, Latifah grilled him about his criticism of the entertainment industry—specifically referring to his wife Tipper's actions with the Parental Advisory Commission.

Queen Latifah's warmth and humor will often allow her to draw more from her guests than others might. That is why she could ask Al Gore (at that time a presidential candidate) exactly how he would protect children from what he saw as harmful entertainment if he were elected, and then turn around and ask him if he preferred action movies or drama (action), or folk or funk music (folk).

The format of famous stars alternating with the appearances of regular people, some of whom are desperately needy, accounts for the wide appeal. Latifah focuses on the solutions, bringing in experts, yet always careful lest a guest become too upset. This concern is mostly due to Latifah's nature, and partly due to what happened on *The Jenny Jones* show in 1995. A guest was surprised by a male friend admitting a crush. Two days later the guest shot and killed the male friend. The family of the deceased sued Jones.

Jim Paratore, president of Telepictures Productions (the coproducer of the show), has said of Latifah's ability to host, "Queen Latifah has the innate curiosity and instincts for relating to people [that] you can't teach someone, and the intellectual depth and emotional range it takes to create a truly distinctive talk show. All you have to do is listen to her music, and you know she's got her own voice."

The first season of her show was not without its

difficulties, but in her usual fashion, Latifah did not give up and managed to succeed where many other new talk show hosts failed that year, including Martin Short and Howie Mandel. Occasionally guests would not show up and she and the staff would have to throw something together at the last minute. Latifah learned a lesson that she had learned many times before, that not everything falls into place right away when starting something new. It takes work, and that is something from which Latifah has never shied.

She wants her show to focus on solutions, and works to keep it that way. "My show is not sleazy at all; it's not tacky; it's not negative. It comes down to execution. We may talk about the same subject, but I really have a mission," she says in response to being compared to shows like *Jerry Springer*.

The impact of her words, her actions, and her movie roles is something Latifah keeps in the fore-front of her mind. While she has made some tremendous mistakes in her life, she has always taken responsibility and owned up to her actions. In her autobiography she stresses that there are definitely things she wishes she had not done, but that as a self-proclaimed queen, she chooses to learn from her mistakes and grow. She encourages others to do the same—not to beat themselves up but rather, pull themselves up and move forward, as she has done and continues to do:

> My capabilities and my possibilities are endless. I have the potential to create, to heal, to comfort, to love, to be the best me I can possibly be. Once you realize what you can do and who you are, you can relax in the confidence of being you.

Growing up in the projects of Hyatt Court in New Jersey, Dana Owens never allowed herself to stop dreaming. Aside from her personal struggles and obstacles, there were the societal prejudices and attitudes that keep many African Americans feeling

The three-day Newark riots of 1967 (seen here) echoed the economic and social frustrations of blacks living in the city. Today Latifah invests both her time and money in rebuilding a sense of pride and community in the place she grew up.

dejected. In 1967, amidst major turmoil throughout the nation and the Civil Rights movement, riots were breaking out among black communities in many major cities. In Newark, a three-day riot in July of that year erupted after rumors spread of police beating a black man to death. By the third day, the National Guard was called in and at the end close to 1,500 African Americans were arrested and 24 were dead, many of whom were later found to be innocent bystanders.

An exodus of middle-class whites followed in the coming years, taking much-needed tax money with them. When Dana Owens and her family arrived in 1978, 20 percent of Newark's population had left.

The city had elected the first black mayor, Kenneth Gibson, in 1970, but the city was very slow to rebuild. The atmosphere was one of despair, economic depression, and high crime rates.

This environment was Latifah's childhood, yet her mother instilled in her a priceless sense of pride and belief in herself. Because of her background and her will and success at overcoming it, Queen Latifah feels strongly about giving back to her community. To that end, she began investing in businesses as soon as she was financially able, opening a video delivery store first. Since her emergence on the rap scene, she has given substantially in many different ways to the areas in and around Newark.

Her latest venture is a real estate company, a Flavor Unit plan devoted to creating low-rise project housing that resembles townhouses rather than the tall, ominous buildings in which she grew up. She wants to encourage low-income residents to feel pride in their homes as a way to nurture their self-esteem. Her mother manages the company.

The Flavor Unit reaches out to inner-city kids by offering scholarships and internships at the company to teach them to believe in their capabilities. Latifah keeps busy doing work for many charities. She has done significant work for AIDS research fund-raising, taking part in concert tours and other events. She has been a strong supporter of women's athletics, especially the WNBA. She also makes a concerted effort in whatever town or city she visits to go and speak at homes for runaway girls and at children's hospitals. In 1998, for example, Latifah visited children at the University of Chicago Children's Hospital, playing with the kids, signing autographs, and distributing T-shirts.

Always aware of the issue of body image and her own struggles to accept herself for how she looks, Latifah last year modeled for Lane Bryant in their

Eager for every new challenge, Latifah makes her modeling debut at Lane Bryant's fall/winter 2000 fashion show in New York City.

fall/winter 2000 show—a show in which no model was under a size 14. In writing about this issue in her autobiography, she argues, "It's a shame that women feel they have to constantly diet and exercise obsessively. They are using good energy to conform to that mythical standard. Think of all the time and money they could be using for a creative pursuit."

She has also been very involved in Rock the Vote as part of the Hip-Hop Coalition for Political Power to reach out to young black voters. She has had her lyrics studied at Harvard University and Cambridge University, only two of the schools where this occurs as part of courses in black studies. She has delivered speeches at colleges and universities all over the country on topics of race, the music industry, and community relations. In 2000 she took part in a three-day conference at Harvard University Law School about race, police brutality, and community issues, especially the phenomenon of "hip-hop" profiling. Artist Master P, worth over $400 million, was asked to leave the first-class section on an airplane because of the style of clothes he was wearing. Latifah herself has experienced such discrimination, and so felt it was important to take part in the discussion.

She also appeared on the celebrity edition of *Who Wants to Be a Millionaire* in May of 2000 and won $250,000 for The Lancelot Owens Scholarship Foundation. In February of 2001, Latifah took part along with singer Joan Osborne in "Take Back the Garden," the V-Day benefit seeking to end violence against women. The show featured more than 70 celebrities reading selections from Eve Ensler's "The Vagina Monologues" and Latifah ended the show with a rousing performance of her hit single "U.N.I.T.Y."

Flavor Unit Records has recently expanded to include two more labels, Jersey Kids and Ghetto Works, and Latifah is working on a fifth album, much to fans' delight. She appeared on the VH1 special *Behind the Music* in July of 2001. At 31 years old, this amazing woman has accomplished more than most people do in a lifetime, and shows absolutely no signs of slowing down. There are always new goals to be met, new challenges to face, and new messages to be heard. She continues to take part in hearings about rap music and the hip-hop culture, she is an advocate for equal rights for women and for gays and lesbians, and she has not let her voice be silenced by anyone.

You think you're living right
But we know it's nonsense
In case you forgot just
Check your conscience

At show time I blow lines
You don't get yours, I get mine
You show signs you're behind
The Queen Latifah divine
Rule no.1: Don't step across
The line that I drew
Rule no. 2: Don't take credit for something
You didn't do
No. 3: check your heart
Every man has a call
It's time for me to go
But I'll be back, y'all   ["Latifah's Law"]

In June of 2001, Latifah took part in Russell Simmons' Hip-Hop Summit, a three-day summit that culminated in a keynote speech by Nation of Islam leader Louis Farrakhan. The main message of his three-hour talk was to urge rappers to take responsibility for themselves as role models and not incite violence. "A lot of rappers have no idea how important their voice is, how important that message is," Will Smith was reported as saying. Queen Latifah and many of the others in attendance felt the same way, and have continued to illustrate that with their actions.

Queen Latifah has been a rap star, an accomplished vocalist, an author, a record producer, an executive, an actress, a model, and a talk show host, as well as an inspiration to many women everywhere. It is hard to predict what she will do next. Given her history, however, nothing seems impossible. And that is exactly how Latifah would see it. The latest buzz about the star is that she may be starting a family soon.

In her book *Ladies First*, she is open and honest about her desire for children, but also says she may want to wait for her "king." Rosie O'Donnell is mentioned, however, as someone whom she admires who has adopted several children, and has even begun her own adoption agency. Whatever Queen

Latifah decides, one can be sure it will be a decision made with thoughtfulness to her own situation, without worrying about what anyone else might think.

> At some point, you have to gain confidence in yourself. Whatever you want to do and wherever it is you want to go, shoot for it. Listen to that big, loud voice that is inside all of us, guiding us if we will only pay attention.

Dana Owens has been listening, and it is the woman we know as Queen Latifah who has emerged. Whatever new project she takes on, whether it involves music, acting, or her businesses, one can be certain it will be done with grace and dignity. Proud, intelligent, beautiful and, above all, regal, she exemplifies many traits young women find worth emulating.

Joining the New Jersey Performing Arts Center Jubilation Choir, Latifah lifts her voice to help inspire positive values in today's students.

CHRONOLOGY

1970   Born Dana Elaine Owens on March 18 in East Orange, New Jersey

1978   Takes the Muslim name "Latifah"; parents separate, and her mother, brother, and Latifah move to Hyatt Court

1979   The Sugar Hill Gang releases "Rapper's Delight"; she skips ahead a grade in school

1984   Transfers to Irvington High School; forms *Ladies Fresh*, an all-female rap group

1986   Graduates from high school

1987   Drops out after one semester at the Borough of Manhattan Community College to pursue a career in rap; her first song is played on the radio that summer

1989   *All Hail the Queen* is released; performs with the rap collective the Native Tongues

1991   *Nature of a Sista'* is released; appears in Spike Lee's *Jungle Fever* and in *House Party 2*

1992   Appears in *Juice*; purchases home in Wayne, New Jersey; brother Lancelot Owens Jr. dies in a motorcycle crash at 24 years old

1993   Begins first season on *Living Single*; appears in *My Life* with Michael Keaton; *Black Reign* is released

1995   Carjacked by two men, one of whom shoots bodyguard Sean Moon in the stomach

1996   Appears in *Set It Off*; arrested for gun and marijuana possession

1997   Appears in *Hoodlum*

1998   Tours with the Lilith Fair; *Order in the Court* is released; appears in *Living Out Loud, The Wizard of Oz, Sphere*; appears in television series *Mama Flora's Family*

1999   Appears in *The Bone Collector* and *Bringing Out the Dead* (voice of dispatcher); talk show premieres

2000   Takes part in three-day conference at Harvard University Law School entitled "Race, Police, and the Community"; models for Lane Bryant's fall/winter show

2001   Filming *The O.Z.*, a hip-hop remake of *The Wizard of Oz*, also starring Brandy; begins work on her fifth album; appears in VH1 *Behind the Music*

ACCOMPLISHMENTS

Discography

1989   *All Hail the Queen*

1991   *Nature of a Sista'*

1993   *Black Reign*

1998   *Order in the Court*

Filmography

1991   *Jungle Fever*
           House Party 2

1992   *Juice*

1993   *My Life*

1996   *Set It Off*

1997   *Hoodlum*

1998   *Sphere; Living Out Loud*
           The Wizard of Oz

1999   *The Bone Collector*
           Bringing Out the Dead (voice of dispatcher)

2002   *The Country Bears*
           Brown Sugar

Television Appearances

1990   *The Fresh Prince of Bel-Air* (two episodes)

1992   *Hangin' with Mr. Cooper*

1993-98 *Living Single*

1994   *The Critic*
           Ellen

1995   *Mad TV* (host)

1998   *Mama Flora's Family*

1999   *The Queen Latifah Show*

2001   *The O.Z.*
           VH1 *Behind the Music*

Books

1999   *Ladies First: Revelations of a Strong Woman* (written with contributor Karen Hunter)

FURTHER READING

Fernando, S. H., Jr. *The New Beats.* New York: Anchor Books, 1994.

Jones, Maurice K. *Say It Loud: The Story of Rap Music.* Brookfield, CT: Millbrook Press, 1994.

Latifah, Queen. *Ladies First: Revelations of a Strong Woman.* New York: William Morrow and Company, 1999.

Lommel, Cookie. *The History of Rap Music.* Philadelphia: Chelsea House Publishers, 2001.

Rose, Tricia. *Black Noise: Rap Music and Black Culture in Contemporary America.* Middletown, CT: Wesleyan University Press, 1994.

Ruth, Amy. *Queen Latifah.* Minneapolis: Lerner Publications Company, 2001.

INDEX

PICTURE CREDITS

❧

SARAH BLOOM has been writing and reading poetry throughout the Philadelphia area for the past 10 years. This is her first published book. Sarah lives and works outside Philadelphia with her daughter Sophia, one day at a time. The author would like to give special thanks to the English department at Rosemont College for their dedication and encouragement.

NATHAN IRVIN HUGGINS, one of America's leading scholars in the field of black studies, helped select the titles for the BLACK AMERICANS OF ACHIEVEMENT series, for which he also served as senior consulting editor. He was the W. E. B. DuBois Professor of History and Afro-American Studies at Harvard University and the director of the W. E. B. DuBois Institute for Afro-American Research at Harvard. He received his doctorate from Harvard in 1962 and returned there as professor in 1980 after teaching at Columbia University, the University of Massachusetts, Lake Forest College, and the California State University, Long Beach. He was the author of four books and dozens of articles, including *Black Odyssey: The Afro-American Ordeal in Slavery*, *The Harlem Renaissance*, and *Slave and Citizen: The Life of Frederick Douglass*, and was associated with the Children's Television Workshop, National Public Radio, the Boston Athenaeum, the Museum of Afro-American History, the Howard Thurman Educational Trust, and Upward Bound. Professor Huggins died in 1989, at the age of 62, in Cambridge, Massachusetts.

921
LAT

Bloom, Sarah R

Queen Latifah

AREA LEARNING CENTER

921
LAT

Bloom, Sarah R

Queen Latifah

AREA LEARNING CENTER
0101911730667

DATE DUE	BORROWER'S NAME	ROOM NUMBER